THE DEMOGRAPHIC SIEGE

THE DEMOGRAPHIC SIEGE

KOENRAAD ELST

VOICE OF INDIA
New Delhi

First Published: 1998
First Reprint: 2012
Reprint: 2025

ISBN 978-81-85990-50-7

Published by Voice of India, 2/18, Ansari Road, New Delhi – 110 002.
Printed at D.K. Fine Arts, Delhi – 110 052.

Contents

1

Visions of a Demographic Doomsday

1.1. Hindus: The Dying Race

Demography can change the cultural orientation of a country or region by making an originally small group numerically dominant. Thus, demographic success was a decisive factor in the Christian take-over of the Roman Empire: in the first three centuries, Christian numbers grew by 40% per year, due to conversion and to the rejection of birth control (whether primitive contraception, abortion or infanticide).[1] Demographic shifts can lead to violence: in Lebanon, the tilt of the demographic balance in favour of the Muslims, leading to demands of a redistribution of political power shared with the Christians, was one of the causes of the civil war. Hindus ought to know, for they themselves have also done it once: "After years of immigration by ethnic Nepalis, [Sikkim] lost its sovereignty when a Nepali majority chose to be part of India."[2] Finally, a certain demography can lead to self-annihilation: many members of India's Parsi community have resigned to the perspective that their community will soon disappear due to a suicidal demographic self-forgetfulness.[3]

In today's India, demography is a hot item, not just because of the economic and ecological burden of overpopulation, but even more because of the differential between Hindus and Muslims with its real or perceived political implications. One of the classic statements of this concern is *Hindu Sangathan, Saviour of the Dying Race* (Delhi 1926), in which Swami Shraddhananda briefly sketches the problem of demographic decline threatening Hindu survival: "while Muhammadans multiply like anything, the numbers of the Hindus are dwindling periodically".[4]

1.2. Ominous Census Figures

Swami Shraddhananda quotes from the 1911 Census Report (para 172ff.) to show the reasons why the Muslim population is growing faster than the Hindu population, whose percentage of the total population is steadily declining. The Census Director had written: "The number of Muhammadans has risen during the decade [1901-11] by 6.7 per cent as compared with only 5 p.c. in the case of Hindus. There is a small but continuous accession of converts from Hinduism and other religions, but the main reason for the relatively more rapid growth of the followers of the Prophet is that they are more prolific."[5] Follow a number of social customs which encourage the Muslim birth rate, e.g. fewer marriage restrictions and common remarriage of widows, and the Muslim insistence that the children of mixed marriages be brought up as Muslims.

In 1909, on the basis of demographic trends visible in the census results (1881, 1891, 1901), Colonel U.N. Mukherji had projected the rate of Hindu decline into the future in a strictly linear fashion, and calculated logically (if somewhat simplistically) that it would take less than 420 years for the Hindu race to disappear completely from the face of India. This was a "correction" on 1891 Census Commissioner O'Donnell's prediction that the Hindus would die out in 620 years. The series of articles in the

Bengalee of 1909 in which Mukherji proposed his analysis was titled: "Hindus, a Dying Race".

This pessimistic prognosis of the numerical Hindu-Muslim proportion defines the problem to which Swami Shraddhananda (who knew Mukherji personally) tried to offer a solution. One of Mukherji's concluding sentences, "They count their gains, we calculate our losses", became the title of a Hindu Mahasabha pamphlet as late as 1979. If anything, the fever of Hindu demographic pessimism is only rising.

1.3. "Hindus Talking Nonsense"

The Hindu suspicion that Islam is using demography to increase its strength and to wrest territories from Hinduism is a constant theme in Hindu Revivalist writing from at least 1909 till today. The rhetoric is often shrill and exaggerated and the case is wrapped in the wrong arguments, most notably the claim that "Muslims have lots of children because they have four wives". A typical example, referring to the official birth-control slogan, "we are two, our [children] are two", is the following: "For the Hindu the slogan is: We are two, and we have two. The slogan for a Moslem is: We are five and we have twentyfive." Sometimes, outside authorities (the BBC, the WHO) are falsely claimed as confirming the Hindus' worst fears: "The United Nations census projections have indicated that the uncontrolled birthrate of the Moslems of India coupled with huge infiltrations will turn India into a Moslem majority country before the year 2000 AD."

It is, therefore, no surprise that *The Economist* ridicules these demographic doomsday scenarios: "Hindu militants are talking nonsense by predicting that chunks of the country will gain Muslim majorities and then secede". There is no doubt that some of the rhetoric generated by this Hindu unrest about the future is plain nonsense, but it doesn't follow that the proportional decline of the Hindus is mere fantasy. *The Economist* itself acknowledges the numerical gains of the Indian Muslim community, and explains that Muslims are less willing to use birth control, and that the infant mortality rate is lower among Muslims because they are more concentrated in the cities where medical care is better.

For those who dismiss U.N. Mukherjee's reasoning as an obvious and ridiculous case of paranoia, it may be useful to verify this prediction for the subsequent 80 years. Official census data show that the Hindu percentage has declined, and the Muslim percentage increased, in every single successive census in British India, free India, Pakistan and Bangladesh. As we are about to demonstrate in some detail, the demographic trends confirm Mukherji's general prediction of a steady decline, though a quantitative prognosis is more complex than he envisaged.

1.4. Demography: The Facts

Considering the pivotal role of the Hindu Revivalist perception that Hinduism is besieged and that demography is one of the weapons used by Islam against Hinduism, I believe that a meaningful discussion of Hindutva ideology is only possible after verification of this fundamental perception. Indeed, on this verification depends whether we ought to consider the Hindutva movement as a bunch of dangerous lunatics spreading lies and paranoia (a fairly common assumption among India-watchers) or merely a group of realistic people who try to face up to real challenges.

The following table shows the percentage of Hindus and Muslims in British India in every successive census since 1881:

yr.	1881	1891	1901	1911	1921	1931	1941
H.	75.09	74.24	72.87	71.68	70.73	70.67	69.46
M.	19.97	20.41	21.88	22.39	23.23	23.49	24.28

And these are the figures for the Indian Republic:[6]

yr.	1951	1961	1971	1981	1991 est.
H.[7]	84.98	83.51	82.72	82.29	81.8
M.	9.91	10.70	11.21	11.73	12.2

These official figures are not altogether accurate for 1981 and 1991, for Assam was not counted in 1981 and neither was the state of Jammu & Kashmir in 1991. Adjusted on the basis of an estimate for these states, the figures for 1991 become: Hindus 81.54%, Muslims 12.60%.[8] The figure of 12.60% for Muslims in 1991 is confirmed by independent secularist observers on the basis of official data and standard procedures for extrapolation.[9] I will use that figure in preference to the Government figure. This brings the Hindu percentage down to ca. 81.5%.

In truncated India, the Muslim population has grown 2.69% in forty years (from 9.91% to 12.6% in 1951-91), but Muslim leaders like Imam Bukhari routinely claim that the true figure of the Muslim population in the Indian Republic is about 3% higher.[10] There are indeed some problems with the official figures for the Indian Republic, e.g. there is a suspicion that many illegal Bangladeshi immigrants are lying low and avoiding the census personnel because they are used to a regime which is not so lenient with unsolicited immigrants (Bangladesh pushed back the Muslim Rohingya refugees from Myanmar in 1992-93). But for the present discussion, it is probably best to keep these alleged unregistered millions outside our considerations and stick to verified figures. Even without this unknown "dark figure" of unregistered Muslim inhabitants, it is only very slightly exaggerated to say that in the Indian Republic, ever since 1951, "the proportion of Muslims has been gradually but steadily increasing every decade by roughly one percentage point".[11]

All kinds of local and regional data confirm the faster Muslim growth rate. The two provinces with the highest relative population growth between 1981 and 1991 are Kashmir (28%) and Lakshadweep (27%), both with a Muslim majority though in very divergent economic and political conditions; followed by Madhya Pradesh (26%) and Uttar Pradesh (25%).[12] In Uttar Pradesh, between 1981 and 1991, the Muslim percentage rose from 15.53% to 17.33 %, in Bihar from 14.13% to 14.81%, in West Bengal from 21.51 to 23.61%. While in Bihar birth control seemed to have a slight effect in a decrease of the decadal increase from 30.03% in 1971-81 to 29.5% (still more than 5% higher than the Hindu figure) in 1981-91, there was a much larger increase in the decadal increase in U.P. from 29.11% to 36.54%, and in West Bengal from 29.55% to 36.89%.[13]

1.5. Extrapolation

How does all this work out for U.N. Mukherji's demographic doomsday prognosis? Mani Shankar Aiyar, the Congress Party's leading anti-Hindutva polemicist, predicted in 1993 that until at least the mid-21st century, the proportion of Muslims will remain stable "bar a decimal point up or down from time to time, at 11.2 per cent."[14] But even the conservative estimate for 1991 (not yet published at the time of his writing) already refuted his prediction by putting the Muslim population more than 1% higher. In the contest between Mukherji's prediction of a continuous Muslim growth and Aiyar's prediction of a stable percentage for the next sixty years, Mukherji has obviously won.

Other secularist observers admit that "it is true that the growth rate amongst Muslims is higher than amongst Hindus", and have calculated, on the basis of the 1971 and 1981 census figures, that "if both the communities continue to grow at the same rate, Muslims at the turn of the century will account for only 13.55% of the country's population."[15] That constitutes a refutation of the still-recent rumour that Muslims will outnumber Hindus by the year 2,000, but also an admission that the Muslim percentage shows a continuous substantial increase. For the long term, their estimate is: "It will take 316 years for Muslims to outnumber Hindus".[16] Here, the difference with Mukherji is merely one over the exact quantity of time needed to do the job.

The projection just quoted is a strictly linear extrapolation of the Hindu-Muslim differential in the decade 1971-1981. But this approach fails to take into account at least two important factors which we will now consider more closely: the Muslim increase is not linear, but is itself increasing; and there is a large immigration of Muslims from Pakistan and Bangladesh, which can only increase.

1.6. The Long-Term Trend

Ever since regular census operations were started, the percentage of Muslims has grown every decade in British India, independent India, Pakistan and Bangladesh. The only *seeming* exception is Pakistan between 1971 and 1981, due to the official declaration of Ahmadiyas (ca. 3%) as non-Muslims in 1974. We will include the Ahmadiyas in the Muslim category, as they themselves also do.

In the subcontinent, Muslims were 19.97% in 1881 and 24.28% in 1941 when the last pre-Partition census was held. According to the last census (1991), the Muslim percentage in the subcontinent was as follows:

Bangla Desh:	86.80% of	108,760,000, or ca.	94,403,608.[17]
Pakistan:	97.00% of	126,406,000, or ca.	122,613,820.[18]
India:	12.60% of	846,349,050, or ca.	106,639,980.[19]
Total:	29.92% of	1,081,515,050, or ca.	323,657,480.

The Muslim percentage has not only increased, but the rate of increase itself has increased. This is very clear when we take a long-term perspective: in the *fifty* years between 1941 and 1991, their percentage has risen 5.64% (from 24.28% to 29.92%), substantially more than the 4.31% gain in the *sixty* years between 1881 and 1941. At this rate, the Muslims in the Subcontinent must have passed the 30% mark in the mid-1990s and will pass the milestone of becoming more than half the number of Hindus (ca. 32% to ca. 64%) before the census of 2011.

Similarly calculating from the available figures for the three countries, the Hindu percentage had come down to 65.15% in 1991.[20] To evaluate the trend of the Hindu percentage, we must take into account that the pre-Independence census always had a tentative category "tribal" or "animist", variously defined and therefore making odd quantitative jumps (but always between 2.26% and 3.26%), from 2.57% in 1881 to 2.26% in 1941.[21] After Independence, this category was included in the Hindu category. So, putting everything on the post-Independence denominator, we include the "animists" in the Hindu percentage to get a total Hindu percentage of 77.35% for 1881. 71.72% for 1941, and 65.15% for 1991. Here again, we see a long-term acceleration of the observed trend: a decrease of 5.63% in the sixty years between 1881 and 1941, and a larger decrease of 6.57% in the shorter period of fifty years between 1941 and 1991.

So, all the predictions quoted above are far too conservative, for they are based on a linear projection. In reality, the observed trends are accelerating, so Muslims will need far less than 316 years to outnumber the Hindus.

According to Mukherji, the Hindu percentage of ex-British India (including India, Pakistan, Bangladesh and Burma) should now have declined by about 13%, down to 54% of the total. This was too pessimistic, he overestimated the rate of Hindu decline, but in the future the increasing rate of Hindu decline will catch up with Mukherji's estimate.

1.7. Muslim Testimony

A very unexpected prediction which more than confirms this trend is implicitly given by one of those authors who ridicule Hindu fears about the demographic evolution: Rafiq Zakaria claims that to outnumber Hindus, "Muslims will need no less than 365 years"[22], but in another discussion in the same book he complains that according to an all-India governmental survey in 1984, Muslim children were underrepresented among primary school pupils: "the enrolment of Muslim children at the primary school level in the relevant period was 12.39 per cent as against the child population of 16.81 per cent."[23] So, Rafiq Zakaria claims that in 1984, Muslim children in the primary-school age group constituted 16.81% of the total.

This means that approximately by the time this group reaches the median position on the age pyramid of their community (i.e. when the number of people younger than them will equal the number older than them), certainly before 2010 (when they will be in their mid-thirties), the native Muslim population of India, not counting the millions of post-1984 immigrants, will be 16.81% of the total. That is even faster than all the above (admittedly cautious) calculations suggest, as if the religious differential in the use of birth control since the 1960s is having a bigger impact than hitherto assumed.

It gets even more dramatic when you look at it this way: in 1984, a generation of Muslims which was about 12% of the population had produced a generation of children, certainly not more than 30 years younger on average, which constituted more than 16%. This would mean an unprecedented growth rate of more than 4% in less than 30 years, or rather, a growth with over a third of the original percentage (4 to 12). For a little thought experiment: if this differential growth rate is kept constant, we get 16.81% of Muslims in ca. 2014, over 22% in 2044, nearly 30% in 2074, 40% in 2104, crossing 50% in ca. 2125 etc., all without counting the effect of Muslim immigration.

Of course, demographic prediction is a difficult task, which has to factor in many different types of data and influences, so we should not take any amateur predictions too seriously, nor those of specialists paid by political institutions with an interest in popularizing this or that impression about demographic trends. Let us not pin ourselves down on precise predictions but let us not ignore the generally visible trend either. The one general prediction to which the data certainly compel us, is that the Muslim percentage will be increasing at an accelerating rate for at least another generation; and also beyond that, unless the present generation of young adult Muslims brings it procreation rate down to the average Indian level.

1.8. The Subcontinental Context

The subcontinental total shows a faster growth of the Muslim percentage than the official figures for the Indian republic, and should be considered the more important indicator for the long-term evolution, given the increasing spill-over of population surplus from Pakistan and especially Bangladesh. Apart from the millions of Bangladeshis staying illegally in India, there is also an increasing number of Pakistanis overstaying their visas or otherwise settling in India.[24]

In Pakistan and Bangladesh, the Muslim percentage has continually increased, partly by pestering the non-Muslims out, partly by conversions under pressure (pressurizing people to marry their daughters off to Muslims, allocating jobs on conditon of conversion, etc.), and partly by higher birth-rates. Bangladeshi Muslim expansion has already destroyed the Chakmas and other non-Muslim populations in the Chittagong Hill Tracts, with the ethnically cleansed minorities fleeing to India's North-East, there to create friction with the host population. But the most worrying from the Indian viewpoint is not the rise in percentage but the rise in absolute figures: in parts of Pakistan and in the whole of Bangladesh, sheer living space is becoming extremely scarce, and these countries may pursue a policy of pushing their surplus population into India.

Incidentally, in Nepal the breakthrough of Islam (nearly non-existent in the 1970s) is simply spectacular, and is again due in large measure to immigration from Bangladesh. In Sri Lanka, the Muslim percentage is slowly rising by demographics alone.

So, every decade the Muslim percentage in the Subcontinent increases by more than 1%, with the rate of increase itself increasing. In India, the rate of increase in the Muslim percentage is considerable, though lower than the subcontinental total, but is rising faster due to the differential in the use of birth control and the increasing Muslim immigration. In Hindutva circles, this remarkable demographic differential is interpreted as the result of Muslim "demographic aggression".[25]

2

Immigration from Bangladesh

2.1. The Uses of Migration

In the demographic competition, simple procreation is not the only factor. There are cases where Muslims are in a minority and use migration to remedy their minority condition. This does not, of course, mean that all Muslims involved in such migration are conscious soldiers in a demographic offensive ("infiltrators"), but an element of planning may nonetheless be involved, or may arise in certain activist circles once the political potential of an ongoing migration process becomes apparent.

Thus, about the situation in Europe, Bat Ye'or observes: "The Islamicist movement does not conceal its intention to islamize Europe at all. Brochures sold in European Islamic centres explain goal and means, including conversion work, marriages with native women, and especially immigration. Knowing that Islam always started as a minority in the countries it conquered, these ideologues consider the implantation of Islam in Europe and the USA as a great chance for Islam."[26]

The Islamic calendar starts with a momentous migration, that of Mohammed and his followers from Mecca to Medina. The result of this immigration from the Medinese viewpoint was that the city lost its autonomy to Mohammed, who became its dictator and expelled or killed sections of its population.

A recent case of the use of demography in the interest of Islam was on the occasion of the 1994 provincial elections in the Malaysian province of Sabah: "The number of Muslim-dominated constituencies in Sabah has increased from 17 in 1990 to 24 in 1994. The [Christian-led] Parti Bersatu Sabah has accused [the ruling party] of flooding the state with Muslim immigrants from Indonesia and the Philippines. Some estimates put the number of immigrants as high as 800,000", with Sabah's original population numbering 1.5 million.[27]

The situation in India follows the same pattern: higher Muslim birth rate, and migration creating Muslim majorities in strategic places. This is most visible in the problem of illegal immigration from Bangladesh in the 1980s and 90s, the most common occasion for using the term "demographic aggression". In the case of immigration, the intentionality is undeniable but it is not necessarily or at least not exclusively motivated by Islamic concerns: Bangladesh is simply overpopulated and wants to get rid of its population surplus by all means available. Non-Muslim governments would probably pursue a similar policy in similar circumstances.

One factor which makes India the prime target of Bangladesh's demographic dumping policy, apart from its geographical contiguity, is the tough policy of other countries vis-à-vis illegal or even legal immigrants: "At the end of last year, there were still more than 100,000 illegal immigrant workers from Bangladesh in Malaysia. As of early February 1997 they are massively expelled by the Malay Government. (...) Bangladesh has some experience with such disasters: last year already, Saudi Arabia, the United Arab Emirates and Qatar expelled some 50,000 illegal Bangladeshis. (...) Three years ago, the Malaysian Government signed an agreement with the Government in Dhaka agreeing to take in 50,000 new guest workers from Bangladesh. But when more and more Bangladeshis entered the country secretly and started to work without work permit, Malaysia canceled the agreement unilaterally."[28] Against Bangladesh's aggressive policy of encouraging its citizens to trespass against the laws of other countries by settling there without permit, most other countries defend themselves with a non-nonsense policy of cracking down on these infiltrators.

2.2. Refugees and Migrants

Immigration from Bangladesh is of two types. Firstly there are members of the minority communities fleeing occasional waves of persecution or the more general sense of being second-class citizens under the Islamic dispensation.[29] Few Hindus would dispute their right to settle down in India. Secondly, there are Muslims seeking economic opportunities or sheer living space, which dirt-poor and intensely overcrowded Bangladesh cannot offer to the ever-larger numbers of newcomers on the housing and labour market.

Hindu Revivalists are glad to quote unsuspect secular sources to confirm their worst misgivings about Muslim demographic aggression from Bangladesh. A 1992 report prepared by B.B. Dutta for the North-Eastern Congress Coordination Committee meeting in Guwahati looked into both types of immigration and notes:

> Between 1971 and 1981, Bangladesh census records show a reduction of 39 lakhs in the minority population.
>
> Between 1981-89, 36 lakh religious minorities were missing from that country.
>
> In 1972, there were 7.5 lakh Bihari Muslims in the camps in Dacca. As a result of mediation by Saudi Arabia only 33,000 of them were accepted by Pakistan.[30] At present, there are less than two lakhs in the camps, where have the rest gone? (...)
>
> It would be interesting to note that a group of intellectuals in Dacca is seeking to legitimise the

migration of Muslims into the adjoining areas of North East region by invoking the theory of *lebensraum* or living space. A number of Dacca dailies carried articles written on these lines by university professors. They were not at all apologetic about the infiltration. People are sought to be inspired by the hope that one day the north-eastern region will be added to Bangladesh giving it a natural boundary in place of present one which throttles Bangladesh.[31]

So, there is a large emigration of non-Muslims, but there is also a large emigration of Muslims, as exemplified by the case of the Bihari Muslims in Bangladesh, of whom the great majority, feeling unwelcome both in Bangladesh and in Pakistan, have simply returned to Bihar and adjoining areas, whence their parents had left for the promised land of (East) Pakistan in 1947. Moreover, the intentionality of the population shift from Bangladesh to India is expressed quite candidly by opinion leaders in Bangladesh.

The BJP argues that refugees from persecution and illegal economic migrants merit a different treatment, as is assumed in the arrangements for refugee relief of most countries. But secularists see it differently, for "unlike the BJP, the Congress (I) views both Hindus and Muslim from Bangladesh as infiltrators".[32] Terminology is a part of the problem here, with secularists systematically describing Hindu refugees as "migrants" if not "infiltrators", and Muslim illegal immigrants as "refugees".

2.3. An Estimate of the Numbers

Arun Shourie has brought the findings of the police and other Government agencies to the notice of the public. According to an Internal Note prepared by the Home Ministry, "large-scale infiltration has changed the demographic landscape of the borders", and it also affects Delhi, Maharashtra, Gujarat, etc.[33]

By 1987, the number of illegal immigrants in West Bengal alone was ca. 4.4 million, and 2 to 3 million in Assam, so that "large stretches of the border in these states are becoming predominantly inhabited by Bangladeshi Muslims. The simmering communal tension in some of the border areas is one of the manifestations of the effects of large-scale illegal migration of Bangladeshi nationals who have slowly displaced or dispossessed the local population, particularly those belonging to the Hindu community".[34] Moreover: "In the metropolitan cities of Delhi and Bombay not less than 4 to 5 lakh Bangladeshi Muslims have been residing".[35]

The Hindu population in East Bengal had declined from 33% in 1901 to 28% in 1941. It fell to 22% by 1951 due to the Partition and the post-Partition exodus, and to 18.5% in 1961. By 1971, it had fallen to 13.5%, partly due to the 1971 massacre by the Pakistani Army, partly due to intermittent waves of emigration. The 1981 figure was 12.1%. In 1989 and 1990, due to "large-scale destruction, desecration and damage inflicted on Hindu temples and religious institutions"[36], "clandestine migration by the Hindus to India went up".[37]

On top of the continuous trickle of Hindu-Buddhist refugees fleeing discrimination and harassment, the big majority of clandestine immigrants consisted of Muslims seeking "living space". It is very hard to count them, but the difference between the actual Bangladesh population in 1991 and predictions for 1991 based on the birth rate and other data shows that millions of people have disappeared from the radar screen of Bangladeshi census workers: "The net shortfall, according to Bangladesh government projection was between 7.24 and 9.24 million, and according to UNDP estimates it was between 12.24 and 14.24 million."[38] And since 1991, millions more have been added to that number.

2.4. Indian Worries

All the BJP's "genuine secularists" are, in their heart of hearts, worried about the demographic increase of the minorities, but they don't want to admit it in so many words. Thus, in its 1996 Election Manifesto, the BJP warns that because of Bangladeshi infiltration, "various demographic entities are bound to come in conflict" due to "an alarming growth of a section of the population"; already, "a section of the population has grown by almost 100 per cent" in certain northeastern areas.[39] Not wanting to sound anti-Muslim, the BJP avoids being explicit about the "communal" angle.

Even to the extent that the BJP does identify the problem as "illegal Bangladeshi *Muslims*", it dooms itself to an unimaginative (and by now probably unrealistic) solution, viz. to physically push these people back across the border, and then build a hermetic fence around Bangladesh. However, the BJP state government in Delhi, voted to power in 1993 on a platform prominently including a crackdown on Bangladeshi "infiltrators", has totally gone back on this promise. Few people seem to realize that the only *democratic* way to conduct this policy of allowing illegal immigration is to have Parliament pass a law declaring: "Henceforth, India gives up the right to control its borders and the access to its territory", a right which is one of the defining elements of sovereignty. Allowing illegal immigration to continue is an act of contempt for India's democratic laws and institutions.

Even a secularist paper has noticed the seriousness of the problem: "The police say that Bangladeshis are behind most of the robberies, stabbings and other crimes being committed in the capital. Their area of operation includes posh localities in South Delhi where most of them work as domestic help.(...) Scarce job opportunities are thus being hijacked by these foreigners. Pakistan claims to be a great friend of Bangladesh, but it is unwilling to allow even one Bangladeshi to stay on. In fact, Pakistan gunned down hundreds of Bangladeshis who were trying to sneak into its territory. If this is how Pakistan is dealing with the situation, there is no need why we should be so generous. As a first step, India's borders with Bangladesh should be effectively sealed. As for those Bangladeshis who are already in the country, they should be identified and deported. Otherwise, the whole country will be paying a very heavy price."[40]

As against the reassuring view that Muslims can only outnumber Hindus in India in a matter of centuries, the evolution in the North-East suggests that the problem of a Muslim majority will take the form of the successive *Unterwanderung* ("to overwhelm by walking in") of designated parts of India within decades. The demographic evolution is bound to create successive Kashmir-type situations, with local Muslim majorities in a (decreasingly) Hindu-majority republic.

3

The Muslim Birth Rate

3.1. Muslim Fertility

Is there anything demonstrably intentional about this Islamic demographic expansion? In an article seeking to "explode the myth" of Muslim demographic aggression, journalists Namita Bhandare, Louise Fernandes and Minu Jain themselves admit that according to official surveys, "the disapproval of family planning is highest among Muslims", while "the practice of family planning methods in 1980 was lowest amongst Muslims (only 23% of those surveyed practised it as opposed to 36% Hindus)".[41] They further admit that between 1971 and 1981, "the Hindu population was up by 24.15%, whereas the Muslim population shot up by 30.59%". Further, they give the decline in fertility levels in the same period: 20.1% decline for urban and 20.0% for rural Hindus, 18.5% for urban and 17.3% for rural Muslims. This means that the already lower fertility level of the Hindus is declining faster than that of the Muslims.

Let us hear the same indications from an official source: "The total fertility rate (TFR) is 3.4 children per woman. (...) Muslims have considerably higher fertility than any other religious group. Muslim women have a TFR of 4.4, which is 1.1 children higher than the TFR for Hindu women."[42]

The implication of these data is that the Muslim rate of growth in percentage of the Indian population will go on increasing. Instead of extrapolating across centuries, we may make a safer prognosis for the next few decades. It is safe to predict that the 2001 census will show another sharp increase in the rate at which Muslims are demographically catching up with the Hindu majority. It is then that the full effect of the birth control campaigns of the 1960s and 70s will become visible. Given the higher Hindu participation in the birth control effort of the 1960s and 70s, we must now be witnessing a cumulative effect, of a proportionately smaller number of Hindu mothers (born in that period) having in their turn each a smaller number of children than the proportionately larger number of Muslim mothers, on average.

3.2. The Economic Explanation

Unable to refute the Hindu Revivalist perception of a visible and increasing Muslim demographic growth, the journalists retreat to their next line of defence: they admit the fact of Muslim demographic expansion but disconnect it from Muslim identity. They offer as their explanation that it has nothing to do with Islam as such nor with any aggressive designs: it is all due to Muslim poverty, "the reason has to do with economics and not with religion".[43] This is the old Marxist clichè: reduce everything to economic factors. It is still the most common explanation for the higher Muslim growth rate: the average Indian Muslim is poorer and less educated than the average Hindu, and poverty and low education both happen to lead to a higher birth rate.

Baljit Rai, a retired police officer who was a personal witness to India's failure in containing the rising tide of illegal immigration from Bangladesh, refutes this argument by pointing to the birth rate among Kerala Muslims, who have a high level of education and a relatively high standard of living. Mani Shankar Aiyar had claimed on the basis of statewise figures for the southern states that "Muslim birth rates in all these enlightened states are very much lower than Hindu birth rates in unenlightened states like Uttar Pradesh".[44] However, Rai's closer analysis of the figures shows that the Kerala Muslims have a higher birth-rate than the national Hindu average and even than the Hindu average in poor and backward states like Bihar, Uttar Pradesh and Rajasthan: the population growth (+28.74% for 1981-91) in the Muslim-majority district of Malappuram (with female literacy at 75.22%, far higher than among Hindus in the Hindi belt) is more than twice as high as the average for Kerala (+13.98), and well above the Hindu national average (+23.50).[45]

A secularist journalist confirms: "In spite of this 'near total literacy' the population growth rate of Muslims who constitute one-fourth of Kerala's population is as high as 2.3 per cent per year, which is more than even the national PGR [= population growth rate] of 2.11 per annum and is almost double the PGR of Hindus in Kerala itself."[46]

The figures for Kerala exemplify a general rule: at any given level of literacy and economic status, Muslims will have a markedly higher birth rate than their Hindu counterparts, even to the extent of having a higher birth rate than Hindus in a lower educational or income bracket. A secularist journalist, Pranay Gupta, estimates that in Hyderabad, which has a large Muslim middle-class, a typical Muslim family has eight children while a Hindu family has four.[47]

3.3. The Literacy Factor

Ever since the propagation of birth control among the Hindu masses, rich and literate Muslims have more children than poor and illiterate Hindus — the religious determinant overrules the economic determinant. This comes out clearly when we compare with the admittedly high growth rate for the Scheduled Castes: "The high growth rate of Muslims, due to poverty, illiteracy etc., is comparable to the growth rate of Scheduled Castes", writes Ashish Bose; but he himself gives the SC growth rate as 31% for the decade 1981-91 against the Muslim growth rate of 32.8%.[48] True, *some* Muslims fall in the same low-income category as the SCs; but taking into account the Muslim middle-class, some old landed gentry and a lot of guest workers in the Gulf states, the average Muslim income is considerably higher than the average SC income.[49]

Likewise, illiteracy is definitely higher among the SCs than among Muslims. And yet, the Muslim growth rate is still 1.8% higher than that of the SCs. "Even after controlling for the level of education among women, religious differentials in fertility persist. Scheduled Caste women have a higher TFR (3.9) than Scheduled Tribe women (3.6) and non-SC/ST women (3.3)"[50] — all of them considerably less than the Muslim TFR of 4.4.

The same is true for the rural-urban differential: just like in other countries, Indian rural couples have a higher fertility (5.7 for Hindus, 6.2 for Muslims) than urban couples (4.2 for Hindus, 4.9 for Muslims), but this secular determinant of fertility is overruled by the religious determinant, for Muslims are more concentrated in the cities but have a higher over-all birth rate nonetheless.[51]

Incidentally, the source just cited, Mohan Rao, provides an example of the misplaced confidence with which secularists berate Hindu Revivalists as unreliable, mendacious etc. Though riding a very high horse in his denunciation of "communal propaganda", Rao himself makes a conspicuously counterfactual statement: "The Hindu population increased by 0.71 per cent between 1961-71 and 1971-81. The population of Muslims rose by 0.05 per cent, much less than that of Hindus. (...) the growth rates of Hindus will continue to be higher than those of Muslims."[52]

He confuses the figures for the increase in population with the actual population figures. The Hindu growth rate increased between 1971 and 1981, from 23.71% to 24.42% (a finding on which Mani Shankar Aiyar builds a similarly mistaken case against a further Hindu decrease and Muslim increase)[53], but remained far below the Muslim growth rate of 30.85% c.q. 30.90%, so that the effective Hindu percentage decreased (by 0.37%). Moreover, this increase was a freak development in a long-term decrease of the Hindu growth rate due to family planning, and was easily undone by a decrease twice as big (to 22.78%) in 1991.[54]

3.4. The Muslim Growth Rate Worldwide

The same trend as witnessed in India is conspicuous at the international level: Muslim countries are among the champions of demographic growth. The economic explanation for high and low birthrates breaks down when confronted with the figures for Muslim countries: the rich and orthodox Saudi Arabs procreate much faster than the relatively poor but more secularized Turks.

The yearbooks of the *Encyclopedia Brittannica* give a wealth of countrywise data, including the population's doubling-rate, which is a more accurate indicator of effective demographic growth than the birth rate. It turns out that no Muslim country has a markedly lower growth rate than India. Indonesia, Turkey and Tunisia are at about the same level as India, which is already seen by many as a demographic disaster area itself (doubling in ca. 33 years). It is no coincidence that these are the three most secularized Muslim countries.[55] The more Islamic a country, the higher the birthrate: Iran, Jordan, Lybia, Kuwait and Eritrea double their populations in 20 years or less, up to twice as fast as India.[56]

The Arabs are the champions: "In no Arab country does the population increase at a rate lower than 2.5% per year.

In practically every Arab country, more than 4 inhabitants in 10 are youngsters below 15."[57] Pakistan is Asia's fastest-growing non-Arab country, doubling its population every 24 years.[58] No country is known to have a higher birth-rate among non-Muslims than among Muslims, but countries where the opposite is true are numerous.[59] The starkest differential is probably found in the European countries. Thus, to use another demographic indicator, the percentage of the under-25 age group in Britain is 33 for natives, 48 for Indians (mostly Hindus) and Caribbeans, 60 for Pakistanis and 63 for Bangladeshis.[60] A similar indicator for the Subcontinent: the under-15 constitute 46.3% in Pakistan, 45.1% in Bangladesh, and 35.2% in India.[61]

In Belgium, the average native couple (Christian or secular) has 1.7 children, the immigrant Moroccan couple (Muslim) has 3.25 children, i.e. nearly twice as many.[62] About American Islam, a Pakistani observer makes an estimate for the year 2,000: "The US (...) may by then become the 14th or 15th 'largest Islamic country'. Islam, in fact, is the fastest-growing religion in the US". Though the growth is largely due to immigration, he also sees "a higher birth rate" as "a major factor".[63]

3.5. Islamic Government Policies

In Malaysia, where Muslims were only 50% at the time of independence, just enough to declare it an Islamic state, the Government pursues a natalist policy at least as far as the Muslim Malays are concerned (non-Muslims are mostly members of the Chinese and Tamil Hindu minorities). It is only in countries where Muslims are in an overwhelming majority and demographic competition is simply not an issue that Islamic governments and religious leaders, faced with the problems resulting from overpopulation, have made an effort to curb the birth rate.

Iran now tries to encourage a three-children-per-family norm, and prides itself on reducing the yearly increase in population to 1.75%, about half of what it was in the 1980s.[64] But this will not markedly curb population growth in absolute figures for the next few decades: "Although the rate of population growth has come down (...) the girls born in response to Khomeini's call for more Muslims will soon reach marrying age; 45.5% of the population is under 15."[65]

Given the extremely high birth rate in the generation now growing up to become the fathers and mothers of the next two decades (much more numerous than the generation presently in their twenties and thirties and trying to stick to the three-children-per-family norm), even a two-children-per-family norm would still amount to an impressive demographic growth for two more generations. With a norm of three children per family, Iran is not even pursuing a policy aimed at achieving demographic zero growth, but even if it were, it could only achieve it at a much later date, and at a much higher population level, than countries with a more stringent commitment to demographic responsibility.[66]

There is no indication that even one Muslim country will achieve a substantially lower growth rate than India's Hindu community within the next decades.

4

Islam and Birth Control

4.1. Islam Condoning Birth Control

It is routinely assumed in Hindu circles that Islam prohibits family planning. But against the talk of Muslim "demographic aggression", secularists like to emphasize that, unlike Christianity and Judaism, Islam explicitly allows birth control. And this is entirely correct. As Yoginder Sikand argues, "Islam is one of the few religions that allow for birth control".[67]

In the Golden Age of Islam (7th-11th century), various writers freely wrote instructions for birth control, e.g. Al-Jahiz wrote in a book about the animal kingdom: "The difference between human beings and other species is that only human beings practise birth control."[68] Of the four Sunni schools of jurisprudence, the Malikite prohibits abortion altogether, the Hanbalite and Shafiite allow it in the first forty days, while the Hanafite school allows abortion in the first four months of pregnancy. All the schools permit the use of contraceptives. The Shiites consider birth control, in pre-modern times mostly *coitus interruptus*, the normal practice in case of temporary (*Muta*) marriages, "so much so that a man who wanted children had to make a special provision in the Muta Marriage Contract so as not to practise 'withdrawal'."[69]

For this reason, there is a lot of practical advice on birth control in Islamic literature, far more than in the fabled Hindu and Chinese sex manuals. A number of medieval authorities on Islamic law and medicine have written about birth control in a matter-of-fact, non-judgmental way. The greatest Muslim medic, Ibn Zakaria al Razi (Latin *Razes*) has given a list of 176 contraceptive or abortive techniques or preparations, while Abu Ali ibn Sina (*Avicenna*) mentioned several dozen.[70] The Hanafi jurist Ibn Abadin allowed women to use birth control and to have an abortion until the 120th day of pregnancy, even without their husbands' consent.[71]

Even Ibn Taimiya, the 13th-century Hanbali theologian who in most matters is the acknowledged godfather of today's "fundamentalists", permitted the use of contraceptive devices. Ibn Taimiya's argument was based on a paradoxical implication of the doctrine of God's omnipotence: no matter how you try to prevent conception, if God has decided that a child will be conceived, scheming human beings are powerless to thwart His designs. Now, since God can always overrule the plans of man, the use of contraceptives does not *really* interfere with God's designs, ergo it is permitted.[72]

In their innocence, some Islamic apologists use arguments to prove Islam's progressiveness concerning birth control regardless of their negative implications in other respects. Thus, the principal of an Islamic college writes: "Islamic jurisprudence has always allowed the above-mentioned family planning method with slave girls as it is one of its fundamental dictates that a slave girl becomes free the moment she gives birth to a child."[73] So, to keep her in slavery it was allowed to prevent her from getting pregnant, which says a lot about the centrality of the institution of slavery to Islamic civilization.

Even more troubling is the context of the main incident in Mohammed's career which justifies birth control (and is therefore routinely mentioned as proof of Mohammed's progressiveness). Mohammed's men had captured women from Mecca in the raid on a Meccan caravan at Badr (see next para), intending to sell them back to their families for a handsome ransom, but asked Mohammed if they could use them for their sexual gratification. Considering that the ransom would go down if the women were not returned in their original condition, the Prophet told his men that they could freely go and rape them as long as they practised *coitus interruptus* (Arabic *azl*). So, the Prophet condoned hostage-taking and rape.[74] Nonetheless, these two instances of clumsy apologetics do confirm that Islam approves of birth control.

4.2. Islam Prohibiting Birth Control

In spite of this solid tradition of at least tolerance to birth control, there is now a strong countercurrent which objects to birth control and propagates a natalist policy. After attacking "the protagonists of Hindutva" for having "perfected the art of demagogy, deception and venomous communal propaganda" including the "oft-repeated accusations that Islam is strictly opposed to family planning", Yoginder Sikand admits: "Their loud proclamations have been further legitimised by some ignorant and obscurantist *mullah*s, who also assert that Islam and family planning are not compatible with each other."[75] Even the alleged Hindutva propaganda that "Muslims are furiously multiplying as part of a grand Islamic conspiracy to swamp the country and convert it into a Muslim-majority state"[76] is candidly confirmed by these "ignorant and obscurantist mullahs".

Leave alone Urdu pamphlets, a neatly published English book from the impeccably Islamic *Noor Publishing House*

(Delhi), Muhammad Samiullah's *Muslims in Alien Society*, is sufficiently explicit about the demographic designs of contemporary Islam.[77] Samiullah rejects family planning as a Western ploy to diminish the numbers of the Muslim population in order to maintain its hegemony. The core of his argument is that birth control has no sanction from the Quran nor from the example and sayings of the Prophet. Since others have claimed just the opposite, a close reading of the source texts of Islam is needed.

As Samiullah notes, Mohammed sanctioned, even commanded, the practice of *coitus interruptus*, the then most readily available method of birth control, in the aftermath of the battle of Badr, his first great victory which yielded him a number of woman hostages. For the present discussion, the point which Samiullah wants to make is that this guideline laid down by the Prophet was contradicted by the Prophet himself on later occasions. Samiullah recounts a number of *Ahadis* (episodes of the Prophet's life serving as the authoritative basis of Islamic law) where the Prophet opposed this method of birth control.[78]

Thus, after the campaign against the Banu al-Mustaliq, the Muslims wanted to rape the hostages and asked Mohammed whether they should practise *azl*, but the Prophet replied, with reference to the futility of human scheming before God's omnipotence: "It does not matter if you don't do it, for every soul that is to be born up to the Day of Resurrection will be born." Since this (and similar ones) is a later Hadis than the one containing his pro-*azl* injunction at Badr, it overrules the earlier one, at least according to the theological principle that in case of contradiction, the earlier pronouncement is overruled by the later one.[79]

Admittedly, the fact that the Prophet encouraged *azl* on at least one occasion does create some legal room for birth control, and Samiullah concedes that it is explicitly permitted in case the woman is in poor health and could not bear the burden of pregnancy and the effort of delivery. But the main weight of Mohammed's normative opinion, Samiullah argues, is certainly on the side of natalism and against birth-control. Hence the Prophet's prohibition, at least on one occasion, of knowingly marrying a sterile woman; his prohibition of non-vaginal intercourse (another primitive form of birth control); and his strict prohibition of sterilization and of voluntary celibacy.

4.3. Islamic Natalism

Hindu Revivalist authors have dug up some more quotations to support the perception of natalist designs in Islam. K.S. Laḷ quotes Mohammed as saying in so many words: "Marry women who will love their husbands and be very prolific, for I want you to be more numerous than any other people".[80] Ram Swarup quotes the Prophet as saying: "In my Ummah, he is the best who has the largest number of wives."[81] Even a secular Muslim candidly calls it "one of the fundamental tenets of Islam — namely, to multiply the tribe."[82]

Samiullah's point is that as a general policy, the Prophet opposed any behaviour which was demographically wasteful and unproductive. He was less fussy about occasional loss of semen in sterile forms of intercourse than Moses' laws had been, but as a rule he favoured the same natalist policy. Samiullah opines: "Had the monster of 'Birth Control' as an instrument of state policy raised its head in the days of the Holy Prophet, he would surely have declared Jihad against it in the same manner as he waged Jihad against Shirk (polytheism)."[83] And he concludes: "The Qur'an says that 'Children are an ornament of life' and Hadith literature views with favour larger families for the greater strength of Ummah, and as such birth control/family planning cannot be in any way compatible with the Shari'ah."[84]

Samiullah argues, not unconvincingly, that the Sharia position is supported by modern science. He cites findings that both the birth-control pill and vasectomy, once (or still) propagated as entirely harmless, are in fact harmful to the concerned person's health.[85] He also shows that the popularization of the pill and other modern forms of contraception has contributed immensely to freer sexual mores in the West, or what he calls immorality. With all this, Samiullah has put together a battery of Islamic plus secular arguments which are bound to sound convincing to the Muslim masses.[86]

Another Indian Muslim author telling Muslim women to "shun birth control" is Muhammad Imran, whose book is published by the Markazi Maktaba Islami ("Islamic Educational Centre"), Delhi, the leading provider of Islamic schoolbooks.[87] He emphasizes that "birth control should be resorted to only in cases of extreme necessity, such as the wife's ill-health owing to constant births. Imam Abu Hanifa holds it *makruh* (abominable)."[88] He too invokes the authority of Western scientists to dismiss it as unhealthy, and points to its "undermining" effects on morality in Western society.[89]

4.4. The Rabita's Natalism

The Indian Muslim authors quoted are not alone. Thousands of preachers instil the same natalist resolve into their flock, even in countries like Egypt and Bangladesh where this position is actually subversive of the Government's official anti-natalist policies: "Even in overpopulated Egypt the theologians reject family planning, at best they merely tolerate the generally ineffective steps which the Government takes."[90]

The natalist and anti-contraceptive line is even defended by the world's most powerful Islamic organization, the *Rabita al-Alam al-Islamiyya* (World

Islamic League). At the UN Conference on Population in Cairo 1994, a number of Muslim countries joined hands with the Vatican in opposing contraceptives and abortion. On the occasion of this UN conference, the Rabita called a meeting chaired by the Saudi king, where a resolution was passed "against the legalization of abortion (...) against a policy of conceding sexual rights to adolescents and unmarried persons (...) against raising the marriageable age (...) We want to make it clear: the Islamic Sharia is against abortion. (...) We strongly oppose the proposed resolution which pleads for complete equality between man and woman." The resolution also alleges that birth control policies are but a Western ploy to mask exploitative designs, and concludes: "If the world's riches are honestly divided, there will be enough for all, and there will be no reason to limit the number of children."[91]

The Cairo Conference was a bone of contention in the Muslim world. Sudan, Saudi Arabia and Malaysia boycotted the Conference. The Egyptian Grand-Mufti Mohammed Sayed Tantawi defended the Conference against a condemnation of its agenda by Al-Azhar university.[92] Egyptian opposition newspapers attacked the Conference, alleging that its anti-natalist agenda would lead to all kinds of immorality and the undermining of parental authority.[93] Thirty prominent Muslims approached the courts in a failed attempt to have the Conference banned.[94] Islamic spokesmen denounced the UNO plans as a conspiracy against "the Islamic bomb, viz. the exponential increase of the number of Muslims worldwide".[95]

The Sudanese Government denounced the Conference as "a ploy to depopulate the Arab countries [and] to minimize the population increase in the Muslim world", and applauded the statement by a professor of Al-Azhar that the Conference intended to "destroy the Muslim nation".[96] While some Muslims favour a realistic population policy, it is undeniable that others approach the matter in terms of demographic warfare.

4.5. Why Muslim Natalism?

The contrast in the Muslim world between the medieval tolerance of birth control and the modern opposition to it can be explained. First of all, even these medieval writings on contraceptive methods have never preached population control as a general policy. Samiullah is probably right to the extent that he distinguishes between people's private lives, where Mohammed did not prohibit birth control, and public policy, where Mohammed took a natalist position. In practice, birth control as condoned by Mohammed and the medieval Muslim authors was never on such a scale that it endangered the steady increase of the Muslim percentage, if only because there was a constant trickle of converts from the non-Muslim communities. Most importantly, there was a situation of unchallenged Muslim domination, not one of Muslim decline and subservience to other powers, as in the 20th century, nor one of permanent confrontation with a non-Muslim majority as in contemporary India.

Demography is a bigger concern today because Islam is fighting for its survival, if not for world supremacy. Muhammad Samiullah is explicit about the good reason for natalism: "There is no denying the fact that the political prestige and military strength of a country depends upon the size of its population. (...) In the Islamic context greater population has a double significance because one cannot wage an effective Jihad without an expanding population."[97]

We may probably generalize that the demographic ebullience of Muslim communities is for the largest part the innocent and automatic result of, firstly, the age-old desire to see the tribe increase, which Mohammed merely confirmed but did not invent; and secondly, of the status of woman in Islam, which is strongly conducive to her exclusive motherhood. However, in the present geopolitical circumstances, certain powerful Islamic organizations have added to these natural factors a deliberate strategy of strengthening the position of Islam by multiplying its numbers. Though they do not have a monopoly on Islamic orthodoxy, they do influence Muslim collective behaviour to a substantial extent, especially in (what is to Islam) a frontline state like India.

4.6. So, Who was Right?

The Hindu Revivalists are essentially right about the ongoing substantial increase in the Muslim percentage of the Indian population. A realistic extrapolation into the future of present demographic (including migratory) trends does predict a Muslim majority in the Subcontinent well before the end of the 21st century, and a Muslim majority in the Indian Union sometime later, but in some regions much earlier. The demographic differential is not of such a magnitude that Muslims will soon outnumber Hindus in the whole of India; but it is large enough to create Muslim-majority areas in strategic corners of the country, "two, three, many Kashmirs!"

Hindu Revivalists who argue that Muslim have a higher birth rate, that their percentage is growing fast, and that this is the result of an intentional policy on the part of at least a section of the Muslim leadership, are right. It is not just that they "have a point" or that they "deserve a hearing", no: they are nothing less than *right*. Only the exact quantity of the trend is a matter for dispute.

And why stop our conclusion with finding the Hindu position right? The data just surveyed also teach us something about the secularists who have ridiculed and thoroughly blackened the said Hindu position: they are wrong. We have not used any esoteric figures inaccessible to the common man; all these data were at the disposal of the secularists. Yet, some of them insist that the Muslim percentage will remain constant, or that the Muslim increase is proportionate to relative Muslim poverty. The fact deserves to be noted: a whole class of leading intellectuals brutally denies easily verifiable facts, i.e. the accelerating increase of the Muslim and the decrease of the Hindu percentage, and the intentionality behind this Muslim demographic offensive.

5

Hindu Response to the Demographic Challenge

5.1. Some Panicky Solutions

This leaves enough time to do something, assuming that "doing something" is in principle possible and desirable. So, what are the options ? It hardly makes sense to react to this demographic aggression with a Hindu demographic counter-offensive, as suggested by the Puri Shankaracharya, if at all it were possible to surpass the Muslim community in this respect.[98] A similar idea is that birth control should be made compulsory for all, e.g. by enforcing vasectomy on every father of two children.[99]

A sinister alternative routinely imputed to the RSS is the expulsion of all Indian Muslims to Pakistan, "the state which was, after all, created for them". This kind of statement can be heard in speeches by the more extreme wing of the Hindutva organization, e.g. in the popular audio-taped speeches by Sadhvi Ritambhara propagating this position, including the slogan: *"Mussalman ke do hi sthan, Pakistan ya qabrastan"*, "There are only two places for Muslims, Pakistan or the graveyard".

This slogan apparently dates back to the Partition and its massacres, as related to me by eyewitnesses.[100] At that time, the evacuation of Muslims from India was, coupled with an ordered evacuation of Hindus from Pakistan, an entirely serious proposal: all Hindus would vacate Pakistan, and all Muslims would go to Pakistan, leaving only their buried ancestors behind in graveyards in India. The proposal was formulated by Dr. Bhimrao Ambedkar in his *Thoughts on Pakistan* (1940), and meant to save millions of lives (including those yet to be lost in future clashes resulting from Hindu-Muslim co-existence in the respective countries of the subcontinent, esp. India). Today, however, it could only be done by means of extreme violence, comparable in intensity to (but a hundred times larger than) the full-scale civil war which led to the expulsion of the French inhabitants of Algeria in 1962.

Anwar Shaikh, a convert from Islam, offers a political solution: "There is only one solution to this horrendous problem, that is, disenfranchise all Muslims of India. A vote is the right of a patriotic citizen who thinks good of his country and acts accordingly. These people lost their Indian citizenship by dividing their own motherland to create Pakistan."[101] Apart from the questionable desirability of such a disenfranchisement, it is obviously a recipe for civil war, for how long would an ever-larger Muslim community tolerate it?

Perhaps Baljit Rai is thinking along the same lines when he offers the undefined concept *Hindu Rashtra* as a solution: "Hindus, Sikhs, Christians, Parsis, Buddhists and others (Muslims excluded) living in India have no option but to live either in a Hindu Rashtra or Muslim India, i.e. India as Dar-ul-Islam. That is the stark reality."[102] Unfortunately, he fails to explicitate how the declaration of India as a Hindu state would stop the Muslim increase leading to a Muslim majority. Nepal is formally a Hindu Kingdom, yet it fails completely to put up any kind of effective defence against Islamic immigration and Christian proselytization, which are fast destroying the Hindu character of the country.

Some desperate Hindus have advocated the reintroduction of polygamy, e.g. one Ashok Vashisht in Britain pleads for adoption of polygamy to counter the effects of Muslim polygamy.[103] His argument is that Muslim polygamy, even if it does not yield a higher birth rate by itself, is nevertheless a decisive trump card in the Muslim demographic offensive, because it limits the availability of women for other Muslim men and thereby forces them to scout around for non-Muslim women. There is something demeaning about this kind of competition, and it overestimates the demographic use of polygamy vastly (polygamous households are rather few and tend to have a lower number of children per woman). But its main conceptual weakness, as also of the other options mentioned, is that it is predicated on the acceptance of the continued Islamic identity of the Muslims.

5.2. Reconversion

Within the above schemes, the choice seems to be one of simply letting the Muslims take over India as soon as they become numerous enough; or implementing one of the said scenarios of demographic competition or ethnic cleansing. One cannot blame anti-Hindu authors for highlighting such ideas as all too similar to certain forms of xenophobia and racism elsewhere. But rather than shrieking about the horrible plans being concocted in Hindutva backrooms, we should take a look at an established Hindu alternative for these extreme "solutions".

The alternative we mean is not to just shrug it all off and say: but why should anyone object if Muslims become the majority? That is a valid option in theory, but one which is unacceptable to every single Hindu worth his salt. After the treatment which Hindus have received in Muslim-majority states and regions, from legal discrimination in Malaysia to ethnic cleansing in Kashmir and genocide in East Pakistan, aborting any evolution which would turn India into a Muslim-majority state is an agreed policy goal.

The other alternative, the one advocated by a string of activists from Dayananda Saraswati to Abhas Chatterjee, is that Hindus challenge the Muslims' adherence to Islam. In Chatterjee's words: "We consider these alien ideologies to be enemies of our nation. The goal is to bring our minorities back into our nation after destroying the deadly intoxication of these ideologies."[104] This was also the solution offered by Swami Shraddhananda to "save the dying race".

This reconversion may take the form of reawakening some peripheral, superficially islamized communities to their pre-conversion Hindu identity, an approach which has worked in the case of the reconverted Malkana and Meherat Rajputs. But today these semi-Hindu Muslim communities are becoming scarce due to *Tabligh* campaigns and the spread of *Madrassa* education, making the Muslims more Muslim. In the larger picture, even the successes which have been achieved by the reconversion movement may not amount to much, for there have also been conversions of Hindus to Islam.

This leads to considerations of a second approach: educating Muslims about the less than divine basis of Islam to shake well-grounded believers in Islam out of their beliefs. The whole idea strikes modern Hindus as quite foreign to Hinduism, which has come to be seen as an entirely spineless jellyfish, tolerating everything, approving everything. In reality, Hinduism has quite a tradition of debate, including wagers in which the loser agrees to convert to the winner's school of thought; an unusually energetic Hindu may try to revive this tradition.

This polemical approach is much more difficult, not least because it necessitates a profound reformulation of Hinduism in modern terms and the shedding of a lot of superstitious deadwood which Hinduism has accumulated over the centuries. Hindu society is not in a shape to teach others lessons and tell them what is wrong with them; or so Hindus feel. That is exactly how Swami Dayananda understood the situation when he conceived the *Shuddhi* programme together with a reform of Hinduism: re-conversion of Muslims is only possible if it is combined with thorough internal reform, both in the social and the intellectual domains.

Demanding as the project of reconversion may be, it is the only civilized solution to the looming threat of a Muslim demographic take-over of India a few decades from now. Of course, Hindus may be lucky and wake up one day to find that Islam has imploded from within, that the Ayatollahs and the Ulema of Al-Azhar and Deoband are suddenly telling their flock that the whole thing was a mistake. The Hindus were that lucky in the case of Communism, which surprised them with its implosion, so it is really possible; nonetheless, luck rarely comes to those who count and depend on it for their survival. Time has not run out yet, and if Hindus make a start today, they can comfortably organize the salvation of their country from the rising tide of Islam.

5.3. A Secular Afterthought

To a modernist outsider, there is something quaint and unreal about this alternative: either islamizing or hinduizing India. Perhaps this is naive Enlightenment optimism, but I wonder if the present worldwide revival of religious idenuties can at all persist once the information revolution has had its full civilizational effect. As late as the 1960s, Protestants in the Netherlands used to warn each other against the Catholics, who were allegedly planning to take over the country with their high birth rate.[105] The suspicious Protestants were right, for today, Catholics are very slightly more numerous than Protestants in the Netherlands, a state created by a Protestant freedom struggle; only, the two communities together hardly command the loyalty of half the population anymore, for both have lost their adherents at a dramatic rate. Moreover, with the mental secularization of even the remaining Catholics, the idea of a Popish Plot to seize power has become surrealistic.

Like the Dutch Catholics, Indian Muslims should be encouraged to outgrow their religious conditioning, and to explore the spiritual sphere afresh. This will automatically bring them in closer touch with their Hindu surroundings, and help them reintegrate into the society from which they were estranged by Islam.

Notes

1. Estimate given by Rodney Stark: *The Rise of Christianity* (1996); this book has received jubilant reviews in Christian circles because it downplays the factor of suppression of Paganism by Christian emperors and highlights positive factors such as the effectiveness of Christian charity in attracting converts, see e.g. the review by Marcel van Nieuwenborgh: "Toen Nieuwe Testament nog nieuw was", *De Standaard* (Brussels), 27-6-1996.

2. "Etnisch konflikt in Boetan leidt tot vluchtelingendrama" (Dutch: "Ethnic conflict in Bhutan leads to refugee drama"), *De Standaard*, 11-8-1992.

3. Among the Parsis, 36% is over 55, and 25% of the adults are unmarried. Their numbers have plummeted to ca. 50,000, half of what it was in mid-20th century. See e.g. Nergis Dalal: "The Parsis are allowing themselves to die out", *The Times of India*, 20-3-1990; Bachi J. Karkaria: "Dying embers", *Illustrated Weekly of India*, 28-1-1990; and Arnavaz Mama: "Survival strategies", *Sunday Observer*, 7-1-1990.

4. Shraddhananda: *Hindu Sangathan*, p. 99.

5. Shraddhananda: *Hindu Sangathan*, p. 18-19.

6. Reproduced in K.R. Malkani: *The Politics of Ayodhya and Hindu-Muslim relations*, appendix 4.

7. Unlike in British India, the census category "Hindu" here includes the pre-Independence category "tribal" or "animist".

8. Syed Shahabuddin: "Census 1991, Muslim Indians and Sangh Parivar", *Muslim India*, September 1995, p. 386. The estimate for Jammu & Kashmir is based on the assumption of a constant ratio between the religions, which understates the Muslim percentage by ignoring the higher Muslim birth rate and the Hindu emigration from the state.

9. Ashish Bose: "1991 Census data: Muslim rate of growth", *Indian Express*, 9-9-1995.

10. In a letter published in *Organiser*, 15-6-1997, Syed Shahabuddin opines that the Indian Muslims may well be "the largest Muslim community in the world", i.e. larger than the Indonesian Muslim community.

11. Ashish Bose: "1991 Census data: Muslim rate of growth", *Indian Express*, 9-9-1995.

12. Calculated on the basis of province-wise population figures given by Joachim Betz: "Indien", *Informationen zur politischen Bildung* no. 257/1997, p. 31.

13. Figures given in Violette Graff: "L'islam indien ë la croisèe des chemins", *Relations Startègiques et Internationales*, p. 118.

14. M.S. Aiyar: "Sex, Lies and Tushtikaran", *Sunday*, 24-1-1993. *Tushtikaran*: "appeasement".

15. Namita Bhandare, Louise Fernandes and Minu Jain: "A pampered minority?", *Sunday*, 7-2-1993.

16. N. Bhandare, L. Fernandes, M. Jain: "A pampered minority?", *Sunday*, 7-2-1993.

17. *Encyclopaedia Brittannica, Book of the Year 1992*, entry *Bangladesh*, official figure for 1991.

18. UNO estimate for religion-wise percentage given in *Jaarboek 1996* of *Winkler Prins-Encyclopedie*; the *Encyclopeadia Brittannica* yearbooks 1991-96 only give the 1981 figure: 96.7%.

19. Total population figure based on preliminary census data, given in various media, e.g. W.M. Callewaert: "De moslims in India", *Kultuurleven* (Leuven), 1997/3, p. 44. The *Encyclopeadia Brittannica* yearbook 1991 only gives a UNO estimate.

20. This assumes the *Encyclopaedia Brittannica* figure for the Hindu percentage in Bangladesh in 1991, viz. 11.9%, which is probably too high.

21. See in Malkani: *Politics of Ayodhya*, appendix 4.

22. R. Zakaria: *The Widening Divide* (Viking/Penguin 1995), p. 181.

23. R. Zakaria: *The Widening Divide*, p. 146. The survey was conducted by the "High Power Panel for Minorities", with Dr. Gopal Singh as Chairman and Zakaria himself as Member-Secretary.

24. "10,000 Pakistani untraceable after expiry of visas", *Indian Express*, 13-7-1994.

25. Most explicitly in the title of retired police officer Baljit Rai's book *Demographic Aggression against India: Muslim Avalanche from Bangladesh* (B.S. Publ., Chandigarh 1993), about the spill-over of Bangladesh's demographic surplus into India.

26. Bat Ye'or: *Les chrÈtiens d'Orient entre Jihad et Dhimmitude* (Le Cerf, Paris 1991), p. 256.

27. *The Economist*, 26-2-1994.

28. *De Wereld Morgen* (Brussels), April 1997, p. 17.

29. Published information about the oppression of and the violence

against the minorities in Bangladesh is extremely scarce. The most accessible general information can be found in Taslima Nasreen's controversial fact-novel *Lajja* (1993, Penguin 1994); an actual report is *Communal Discrimination in Bangladesh: Facts and Documents*, compiled and published by the Bangladesh Hindu-Buddhist-Christian Unity Council, 1993.

30. Urdu-speaking Bihari Muslims migrated from Bihar to East Pakistan in 1947. In the Urdu-Bengali controversy and in the Bengali freedom struggle they sided with Pakistan, a position which turned them into unwanted refugees after the creation of Bangladesh.

31. "Report 'C' — 1992 of Congress (I)", excerpts reproduced as appendix 2 in Arun Shourie: *Secular Agenda* (ASA, Delhi 1993), quotation on p. 299-300; as annexure B in Baljit Rai: *Is India Going Islamic?* (B.S. Publ., Chandigarh 1994), quotation on p. 91-92; and in S.N.M. Abdi: "No place to call their own", *Illustrated Weekly of India*, 14-11-1992.

32. Statement by Mr. D.P. Roy, joint secreatry of the All-India Congress Committee, quoted by Tapan Sikdar, president of the West Bengal BJP: "How West Bengal Congress is providing fillip to Muslim infiltrators", *BJP Today*, 1-10-1992.

33. Appendix 1 in Arun Shourie: *A Secular Agenda*, spec. p. 269.

34. In Shourie: *Secular Agenda*, p. 269-270.

35. In Shourie: *Secular Agenda*, p. 270.

36. A list of over 200 Hindu places of worship attacked or destroyed in November 1989, compiled by the Hindu-Buddhist-Christian Unity Council of Bangladesh, is given in Shourie, Goel et al.: *Hindu Temples, What Happened to Them*, vol. 1 (Voice of India 1990), appendix.

37. Shourie: *Secular Agenda*, p. 272.

38. Internal Note, in Shourie: *Secular Agenda*, p. 273.

39. *BJP Election Manifesto 1996*, p. 39. Though intended as quite serious, this could practically be read as a parody of the Press Council rules pertaining to riot reporting (where "Muslims burned a temple down" becomes "members of a particular community damaged a religious building"). BJP spokesmen have tried to justify this wording with reference to a crackdown on Hindu refugees by the CPM Government of West Bengal, who wanted to show that Hindus would suffer first if anything was undertaken against Bangladeshi immigrants.

40. Rajiv Shukla: "The unwanted guests. Isn't it time we sorted out the Bangladeshi illegal immigrants issue?", *Sunday*, 12/2/1995.

41. "A pampered minority?", *Sunday*, 7-2-1993, with reference to a 1980 survey by the Operations Research Group.

42. K.M. Mathew, ed.: *Manorama Yearbook* 1996, p. 458-459.

43. "A pampered minority?", *Sunday*, 7-2-1993.

44. M.S. Aiyar: "Sex, Lies and Tushtikaran", *Sunday*, 24-1-1993.

45. See Baljit Rai: *Is India Going Islamic?*, p. 103ff.

46. K.B. Sahay: "Incentives and Disincentives", *Hindustan Times*, 19/12/1995.

47. P. Gupta: *India, the Challenge of Change* (Methuen/Mandarin, London 1989), p. 219.

48. A. Bose: "Muslim rate of growth", *Indian Express*, 9-9-1995.

49. As Ashish Bose regretfully notes, the 1991 census gives no cross-tabulation between the data on religion, income and literacy, so we have to make do with old data, informed guesses or separate regional investigations into the connections between these factors.

50. K.M. Mathew, ed.: *Manorama Yearbook* 1996, p. 458-459. TFR: total fertility rate.

51. Figures given in Mohan Rao: "Not born of faith", *Indian Express*, 9-11-1993.

52. M. Rao: "Not born of faith", *Indian Express*, 9-11-1993.

53. M.S. Aiyar: "Sex, Lies and Tushtikaran", *Sunday*, 24-1-1993.

54. "Census 1991", in S. Shahabuddin, ed.: *Muslim India*, Sep. 1995, p. 386.

55. Mohan Rao ("Not born of faith", *Indian Express*, 9-11-1993) argues that "the percentage of couples using contraceptives in predominantly Muslim countries is very high", and to prove his point, he cites figures for Indonesia, Turkey and Egypt, three countries where the Government policies are denounced as *un-Islamic* by the guardians of orthodoxy.

56. Figures taken from the countrywise data in the *Encyclopedia Brittannica Book of the Year 1994*.

57. "Arababy's", *Trends* (Brussels), 6-9-1990.

58. Confirmed in a different set of demographic indicators given in *The Economist*, 3-10-1992.

59. The only countries competing with the top Muslim countries for the highest demographic growth rate are some African countries (Kenya, Ivory Coast); at least on paper, for their projected doubling-time will have to be revised downwards because of the AIDS epidemic.

60. Figures given by Prof. Judith Brown, Beit Professor of Imperial History, Oxford, speaking at the Annual South Asia Conference, Madison, Wisconsin, October 1995.

61. *Encyclopedia Brittannica*, 1996 yearbook.

62. Guy Tegenbos: "Gezinnen kroostrijkst bij Marokkanen en Israîlieten", *De Standaard*, 17-8-1994.

63. Abdus Sattar Ghazali: "Middle East poised to confront demographic explosion", *Dawn* (Karachi), 3-11-1989.

64. "Iran brengt groei bevolking sterk terug" (Dutch: "Iran strongly reduces population growth"), *Volkskrant* (Amsterdam), 13-7-1995.

65. "Arrows in the heart of Iran", *The Economist*, 3-10-1992. The title is a pun on Ayatollah Khomeini's natalist exhortation that "every Muslim child born is an arrow through the heart of America".

66. E.g. Vietnam, with a two-children-per-family norm but still increasing by over 1 million per year, not to speak of China with its draconic one-child-per-family norm but a population still increasing at a rate of over 10 million individuals per year.

67. Yoginder Sikand: "Bogey of family planning and Islam", *Observer of Business and Politics*, 27-2-1993, with reference to B.F. Musallam: *Sex and Society in Islam* (Cambridge 1933).

68. Quoted in Lucas Catherine: *Islam voor Ongelovigen* (EPO, Antwerp 1997), p. 215.

69. Yoginder Sikand: "Bogey of family planning and Islam", *Observer of Business and Politics*, 27-2-1993.

70. Quoted in Lucas Catherine: *Islam voor Ongelovigen*, p. 216.

71. Quoted to this effect by Yoginder Sikand: "Bogey of family planning and Islam", *Observer of Business and Politics*, 27-2-1993.

72. Quoted to this effect by L. Catherine: *Islam voor Ongelovigen*, p. 216.

73. Wasi Ahmad Siddiqi: "Family Planning and Prophet", letter in *Indian Express*, 30-4-1990.

74. Though Ram Swarup discusses this and similar episodes (*Understanding Islam through Hadis*, p. 61-62, ref. to *Sahih al-Muslim* 3371), he does not draw attention to this revealing aspect pertaining to Islamic ethics.

75. Yoginder Sikand: "Bogey of family planning and Islam", *Observer of Business and Politics*, 27-2-1993.

76. Yoginder Sikand: "Bogey of family planning and Islam", *Observer of Business and Politics*, 27-2-1993.

77. Muhammed Samiullah: *Muslims in Alien Society* (Delhi 1992), esp. ch. 8: "Islam and Birth Control", p. 86-97.

78. Samiullah: *Muslims in Alien Society*, p. 87.

79. This exegetical principle (called *nashk*) is disputed by some progressive theologians. Thus, concerning the relations with non-Muslims, the older verses are more restrained while later verses are very combative; but Mahmud Shaltut, Rector of Al-Azhar in 1958-63 (*Koran and Fighting*, reproduced in R. Peters: *Jihad in Classical and Modern Islam*, Markus Wiener, Princeton 1997, esp. p. 80-82) rejects the view that the more peaceful verses stand abrogated by the later, more warlike ones. His argument is that all of them are divinely revealed and therefore valid; it is up to the interpreter to rhyme seemingly contradictory verses together, rather than arrogantly declaring some of God's verses invalidated.

80. Quoted from T.P. Hughes: *Dictionary of Islam*, p. 314, who refers to book 13 of *Mishkatu'l Masabih* ("niches for lamps [of the tradition]", a compilation of Sunni traditions by the 12th-century Imam Husain al-Baghawi, expanded in the 14th century by Shaykh Waliuddin).

81. Katib al-Waqidi (= Ibn Sa'd): *Tabqat Ibn Sa'd*, vol. 2, p. 146 of the

Urdu translation from Nafees Academy, Karachi; quoted by Ram Swarup: *Understanding Islam through Hadis* (Voice of India 1989), p. 57n.

82. Saeed Naqvi: *Reflections of an Indian Muslim* (Har-Anand, Delhi 1993), p. 32.

83. M. Samiullah: *Muslims in Alien Society*, p. 90.

84. M. Samiullah: *Muslims in Alien Society*, p. 97.

85 See e.g. Dr. Ellen Grant: *The Bitter Pill* (Elm Tree Books, London 1985), which presents the (grim) medical case against the birth-control pill.

86. That this natalist position has struck roots among ordinary Muslims may be illustrated with the case of Mohammed Tofazzal Mollah: he was sacked as Imam at the village mosque of Bahipara (northern Bangladesh) because his wife had been sterilized after having given birth to six children. The village population rallied behind the two Maulanas who had issued the *fatwa* condemning the poor Imam. See: "Imam faces fatwa as wife refuses to conceive", *Indian Express*, 18-11-1993.

87. M. Imran: *Ideal Woman in Islam*, Delhi 1994 (1981), p. 66.

88. M. Imran: *Ideal Woman in Islam*, p. 66.

89. M. Imran: *Ideal Woman in Islam*, p. 68.

90. "Iranische Theologen flr Geburtenkontrolle" (German: "Iranian theologians in favour of birth control"), *Frankfurter Allgemeine Zeitung*, 19-1-1990. The main thrust of the article is that in Iran's Islamic Republic, the theologians are more loyal to the regime and its policies (i.c. the switch from a natalist to a moderately anti-natalist policy), while in Egypt, they take a doctrinaire Islamic line against the "secular" Government policies.

91. Mecca, 3-9-1994, quoted in L. Catherine: *Islam voor Ongelovigen*, p. 217.

92. "Kairo-konferentie verdeelt moslims" (Dutch: "Cairo Conference divides Muslims"), *De Morgen* (Brussels), 24-8-1994.

93. "Egyptische islamisten verwerpen konferentie" (Dutch: "Egyptian Islamists reject conference"), *De Standaard*, 17-8-1994.

94. "Rechter weigert konferentie te verbieden" (Dutch: "Judge refuses to prohibit conference"), *De Morgen*, 31-8-1994.

95. "'Vrouwen zijn sleutel voor de ontwikkeling'" (Dutch: "'Women are key to development'"), *De Morgen*, 17-8-1994.

96. "'Westerse delegaties zullen ernstige risico's lopen': Khartoem waarschuwt VN-bevolkingskonferentie in Kairo" (Dutch: "'Western delegations will run serious risks': Khartum warns UN Conference in Cairo"), *De Morgen*, 27-8-1994.

97. M. Samiullah: *Muslims in Alien Society*, p. 95-96.

98. The Shankaracharya was quoted to this effect in *India Today*, 31-5-1986, with the comment: "Hindu stalwarts like him are convinced — however ludicrous it might sound — that a conspiracy of sociology and demography will soon render the Hindus a minority in their own country."

99. Not that this is so extreme, for even model secularist Khushwant

Singh writes (*Need for a New Religion in India and Other Essays*, UBSPD, Delhi 1993, p. 16): "We must disenfranchise parents who have more than two children and forbid them from holding elective offices. We must also make sterilisation of both parents on the birth of their second child compulsory."

100. Including Madanlal Pahwa, a refugee from West Pakistan and an accomplice in the Mahatma Gandhi murder case, whom I interviewed in Mumbai, January 1996.

101. Anwar Shaikh: *Is India Going Islamic? — a Review* (private pamphlet reviewing Baljit Rai's book, Cardiff 1994), p. 8. In his latest book (*A Tale of Two Gujarati Saints*, A. Ghosh, Houston 1998), he explicitly abandons this position.

102. Baljit Rai: *Is India Going Islamic?*, p. 107

103. A. Vashisht: "Marriage game: beat the Mussalman", *Young India*, July 1995.

104. A. Chatterjee: *Hindu Nation* (Voice of India, 1995), p. 45.

105. And as late as 1976, my schoolteacher of Catholic religion told us to have many children, for this was the way to make the Catholic community stronger and more powerful. On present trends, the Catholic minority in Northern Ireland is all set to numerically overtake the Protestant majority.